The Ultimate Book of Inspiring Quotes for Kids

Michael Stutman and Kevin Conklin

ISBN: 1512330132
ISBN 13: 978-1512330137
Library of Congress Control Number: 2015908297

For our children—Ryan, Anna, Daniel, Sean, Jason, Andrew, and Lily—who inspired the InspireMyKids journey and make it real for us every day.

For our wives, Karen and Emily, who lovingly remind us to live these virtues every day and have supported our journeys from day one.

For our parents—Bill, Nancy, Walter, and Joan—who taught us the importance of these values and gave us solid foundations to build from.

For our mentors—Johnna, Chris, Sharol, and Haylie—for helping to light the spark and continuing to fuel it with their encouragement and feedback.

For the authors of the quotes in this book, for sharing their immense wisdom with the world.

We thank you all from the bottoms of our hearts.

Mike and Kevin

INTRODUCTION

A Note to Children

Becoming the best version of yourself, keeping a positive attitude, and helping to change the world for the better are no easy tasks! They take inspiration, encouragement, wisdom, and good habits.

Quotes can be an incredible fuel for your fire. They can shine a light on new ways of thinking, reveal how successful people handle different situations, and inspire you in a fast and fun way.

If you look at the quotes on the pages that follow, you will see that many of them come from people who have made big differences in the world. This is not a coincidence. It was not only their cleverness that helped them stand out and change the world but also their values and habits. This book focuses on these habits and can help you shape your thinking, values, and actions.

Use the words in this book to inspire your own version of greatness. If you can work to develop the same habits and thinking that appear in these pages, it will not just a great benefit to you, but also to your family, career, school, and community.

The good news is that even small actions and small changes to the way you think can have a huge impact on your life and the world. So don't wait! Start today—get inspired, and practice taking positive actions every day. Instead of just thinking about doing the right thing, do the right thing. Keep doing good things, and soon they will become habits.

INTRODUCTION

A Note to Adults & Educators

The inspiring words and people found in this book are at the heart of what we do at InspireMyKids.

Our unwavering goal is to share inspiring, age-appropriate, real-life stories, quotes, media, and projects that help children become the best they can be and take positive action to make the world a better place.

We have focused this collection of quotes on topics that matter to the development of character in children. We selected quotes based on their potential appeal to children and then validated based on feedback by children.

Whether you are an educator, parent, coach or mentor, we trust you will find inspiration in these pages. Thank you for your desire to make the world a better place.

We also hope that you will join us on the InspireMyKids (IMK) journey at our home–the world's largest community of inspiration for kids– www.inspiremykids.com.

Mike Stutman and the IMK Team

Co-founder and Dad

www.inspiremykids.com

mike@inspiremykids.com

TABLE OF CONTENTS

InspireMyKids.com

BRAVERY & STRENGTH

You know bravery when you see it. Bravery can be as simple as sleeping over at a friend's house for the first time, even when you are scared to do so. It can be standing up for someone in his or her time of need. It can be as difficult as undergoing years of painful medical treatments.

Being brave makes you better at everything that you do, whether it enables you to participate more in class, speak in public, or try a new sport or activity. In fact, developing bravery–little by little–is one of the best things you can do to set yourself up for success in life.

Many of the people who have had the greatest impact on the world have exhibited bravery. From Abraham Lincoln to Nelson Mandela, bravery was at their core.

Here are some great quotes on the topic of bravery and strength:

"We are only as strong as we are united, as weak as we are divided"

– J. K. Rowling

"You have power over your mind—not outside events. Realize this, and you will find strength"

— Marcus Aurelius

"With the new day comes new strength and new thoughts"

— Eleanor Roosevelt

"Be strong. Live honorably and with dignity. When you don't think you can, hold on"

— James Frey

"The golden rule is that to act fearlessly upon what one believes to be right"

— Mahatma Gandhi

"Success is not final, failure is not fatal: it is the courage to continue that counts"

— Sir Winston Churchill

"It's not the size of the dog in the fight, it's the size of the fight in the dog"

— Mark Twain

InspireMyKids.com

"I learned that courage was not the absence of fear, but the triumph over it. The brave man is not he who does not feel afraid, but he who conquers that fear"

– Nelson Mandela

"Being brave is when you have to do something because you know it is right, but at the same time, you are afraid to do it because it might hurt or whatever. But you do it anyway"

– Meg Cabot

"When a brave man takes a stand, the spines of others are often stiffened"

– Billy Graham

"The future doesn't belong to the light-hearted. It belongs to the brave"

– Ronald Reagan

"He who is brave is free"

– Seneca

"Heroes are people who face down their fears. It is that simple"

– David Gemmell

InspireMyKids.com

"He doesn't need to be big to be brave, because bravery is the courage found in the heart"

– Aishah Madadiy

CARING & KINDNESS

Caring and kindness—two very simple words, but two actions that can change your world and the world around you. They are qualities that, when you practice them, bring happiness not only to others but back to you as well.

Every day we have many choices to make in the way we treat other people and the world around us. These little choices add up to big things: they define who we are as people.

To inspire you in your own efforts to be more caring and kind, here are some quotes that describe how important these virtues can be to you and others:

"Never believe that a few caring people can't change the world. For, indeed, that's all who ever have"

– Margaret Mead

"What this world needs is a new kind of army—the army of the kind"

– Cleveland Armory

"The simple act of caring is heroic"

— Edward Albert

"No act of kindness, no matter how small, is ever wasted"

— Aesop

"I feel the capacity to care is the thing which gives life its deepest significance"

— Pablo Casals

"You cannot do a kindness too soon, for you never know how soon it will be too late"

— Ralph Waldo Emerson

"Wherever there is a human being, there is an opportunity for kindness"

— Seneca

"Unless someone like you cares a whole awful lot, nothing is going to get better. It's not"

— Dr. Seuss

"Always stop to think whether your fun may be the cause of another's unhappiness"

— Aesop

"Of all virtues and dignities of the mind, goodness is the greatest"

– Francis Bacon

"Choose being kind over being right and you'll be right every time"

– Richard Carlson

"Goodness is the only investment that never fails"

– Henry David Thoreau

"That best portion of a man's life, his little, nameless, unremembered acts of kindness and love"

– William Wordsworth

"If you see someone without a smile, give them one of yours"

– Dolly Parton

"They're only truly great who are truly good"

– George Chapman

"Do to others as you would have them do to you"

– The Bible: Luke 6:31

"You can't live a perfect day without doing something for someone who will never be able to repay you"

— John Wooden

"If you judge people, you have no time to love them"

— Mother Teresa

"Never look down on anybody unless you're helping him up"

— Jesse Jackson

"The kindest word in all the world is the unkind word, unsaid"

— Anonymous

"Your greatness is measured by your kindness"

— William Boetcker

"You are not only responsible for what you say, but for what you do not say"

— Martin Luther

"Fashion your life as a garland of beautiful deeds"

— Buddha

InspireMyKids.com

"Forget injuries; never forget kindness"

– Confucius

"When I was young, I admired clever people. Now that I am old, I admire kind people"

– Abraham Joshua Heschel

"When you are kind to others, it not only changes you, it changes the world"

– Harold Kushner

"Always be a little kinder than necessary"

– J.M. Barrie

"Kind words can be short and easy to speak, but their echoes are truly endless"

– Mother Teresa

COURAGE

Have you ever done something that you knew was the right thing to do, but you were scared to do it? Or maybe you did something that looked very hard, but you decided to try it. That is courage in action, and you probably felt very good about what you did. And you should!

Courage shows up in many ways all around you. Courage is standing up for a friend, helping someone in need, or sticking with something that is hard for you to do. Courage is one of the most important things you can develop as a young person. Having courage makes you a better person, a better student, and a better citizen.

Here are some great quotes on the topic of courage:

"Courage is doing what you're afraid to do. There can be no courage unless you're scared"

– Edward Vernon Rickenbacker

"Courage is resistance to fear, mastery of fear—not absence of fear"

– Mark Twain

"One of the greatest discoveries a man makes, one of his great surprises, is to find he can do what he was afraid he couldn't do"

— Henry Ford

"It takes courage for people to listen to their own goodness and act on it"

— Pablo Casals

"He is courageous who endures and fears the right thing, for the right motive, in the right way and at the right times"

— Aristotle

"The greatest mistake you can make in life is to be continually fearing that you will make one"

— Elbert Hubbard

"A hero is no braver than an ordinary man, but he is braver five minutes longer"

— Ralph Waldo Emerson

"You gain strength, courage, and confidence by every experience in which you really stop to look fear in the face. You must do the thing you think you cannot do"

— Eleanor Roosevelt

InspireMyKids.com

"Success is not final, failure is not fatal: it is the courage to continue that counts"

– Sir Winston Churchill

"Courage is never to let your actions be influenced by your fears"

– Arthur Koestler

"Life shrinks or expands in proportion to one's courage"

– Anais Nin

"To dream anything that you want to dream. That's the beauty of the human mind. To do anything that you want to do. That is the strength of the human will. To trust yourself to test your limits. That is the courage to succeed"

– Bernard Edmonds

"All our dreams can come true...if we have the courage to pursue them"

– Walt Disney

"Trust the still, small voice that says, 'this might work and I'll try it'"

– Diane Mariechild

"Man cannot discover new oceans unless he has the courage to lose sight of the shore"

– André Gide

InspireMyKids.com

"The greatest test of courage on earth is to bear defeat without losing heart"

– Robert Green Ingersoll

"Life is not meant to be easy, my child; but take courage—it can be delightful"

– George Bernard Shaw

"Courage is what it takes to stand up and speak; courage is also what it takes to sit down and listen"

– Winston Churchill

"Courage doesn't always roar. Sometimes courage is the little voice at the end of the day that says I'll try again tomorrow"

– Mary Anne Radmacher

"Have the courage to say no. Have the courage to face the truth. Do the right thing because it is right. These are the magic keys to living your life with integrity"

– W. Clement Stone

"It may take courage to embrace the possibilities of your own potential, but once you've flown past the summit of your fears, nothing will seem impossible"

– Michael McKee

InspireMyKids.com

EDUCATION & LEARNING

Education and learning are two of the most important ingredients to becoming all that you can be. How open you are to learning will help determine your path in life.

Education does not just happen at school. It is not just about math and other subjects. Learning is happening all the time, whenever your mind is open.

Education is not just about learning facts but more so about learning how to think. It is learning to make good choices. It is learning to act with purpose.

Becoming educated is a lifelong process. It can be hard and frustrating at times, but it can also be incredibly exciting and enriching. Most importantly, learning and education can help you to achieve the following:

- Change the world
- Become your best self
- Reach your potential
- Eliminate your fears
- Make the most of your mistakes
- Support your family

Here are some inspiring quotes that capture the power of education and its potential to impact you and the world:

"Education is the most powerful weapon which you can use to change the world"

– Nelson Mandela

"When you know better you do better"

– Maya Angelou

"Somewhere, something incredible is waiting to be known"

– Carl Sagan

"Even the wisest mind has something yet to learn"

– George Santayana

"Anyone who stops learning is old, whether at twenty or eighty. Anyone who keeps learning stays young"

– Henry Ford

"The important thing is not to stop questioning"

– Albert Einstein

InspireMyKids.com

"Learning is a treasure that will follow its owner everywhere"

– Chinese proverb

"None of us is as smart as all of us"

– Ken Blanchard

"A house is not a home unless it contains food and fire for the mind as well as the body"

– Benjamin Franklin

"The mind is not a vessel to be filled, but a fire to be kindled"

– Plutarch

"Educating the mind without educating the heart is no education at all"

– Aristotle

"You can tell whether a man is clever by his answers. You can tell whether a man is wise by his questions"

– Naguib Mahfouz

"Education is not the filling of a pail, but the lighting of a fire"

– W. B. Yeats

InspireMyKids.com

"If you can't explain it simply, you don't understand it well enough"

— Albert Einstein

"Nothing in life is to be feared. It is only to be understood"

— Marie Curie

"A mistake is a crash-course in learning"

— Billy Anderson

"We are not what we know but what we are willing to learn"

— Mary Catherine Bateson

"He who opens a school door, closes a prison"

— Victor Hugo

"Knowledge will bring you the opportunity to make a difference"

— Claire Fagan

"Education is teaching our children to desire the right things"

— Plato

"I believe that we learn by practice. Whether it means to learn to dance by practicing dancing or to learn to live by practicing living, the principles are the same. Practice means to perform, over and over again in the face of all obstacles, some act of vision, of faith, of desire. Practice is a means of inviting the perfection desired"

— Martha Graham

"Education is the power to think clearly, the power to act well in the world's work, and the power to appreciate life"

— Brigham Young

"I received the fundamentals of my education in school, but that was not enough. My real education, the superstructure, the details, the true architecture, I got out of the public library. For an impoverished child whose family could not afford to buy books, the library was the open door to wonder and achievement, and I can never be sufficiently grateful that I had the wit to charge through that door and make the most of it"

— Isaac Asimov

"Painful as it may be, a significant emotional event can be the catalyst for choosing a direction that serves us—and those around us—more effectively. Look for the learning"

— Louisa May Alcott

"Imagination is more important than knowledge. For knowledge is limited to all we now know and understand, while imagination embraces the entire world, and all there ever will be to know and understand"

– Albert Einstein

EMPATHY

Empathy is trying to understand what another person is feeling. It is seeing the world through another's eyes. It helps people to get along better and to feel better.

Having empathy is a key ingredient to becoming the best person you can be. Here are some ideas to practice empathy:

- Listen to people rather than trying to talk to them

- Ask others how they are feeling if you think there is something wrong

- Learn about people from different backgrounds and cultures

- Show concern and care for others

- Pay attention to the needs of others

- Get to know people better instead of judging them

Empathy is easy to say but hard to do. The quotes below talk about the importance of empathy in the world. Learn about empathy and practice it in your life. The world will be a better place because of you!

InspireMyKids.com

"Empathy is seeing with the eyes of another, listening with the ears of another and feeling with the heart of another"

— Alfred Adler

"You can only understand people if you feel them in yourself"

— John Steinbeck

"If you judge people, you have no time to love them"

— Mother Teresa

"We judge what we don't understand"

— Anonymous

"The opposite of anger is not calmness. It's empathy"

— Mehmet Oz

"If you see someone without a smile, give them one of yours"

— Dolly Parton

"I believe empathy is the most essential quality of civilization"

— Roger Ebert

"Empathy grows as we learn"

— Alice Miller

"Never look down on anybody unless you're helping him up"

— Jesse Jackson

"The purpose of human life is to serve, and to show compassion and the will to help others"

— Albert Schweitzer

"No one cares how much you know, until they know how much you care"

— Theodore Roosevelt

"We have two ears and one mouth so that we can listen twice as much as we speak"

— Epictetus

"Don't cast shadows on anyone unless you are providing shade"

— Terri Guillemets

"There is no greater loan than a sympathetic ear"

— Frank Tyger

InspireMyKids.com

"When I get ready to talk to people, I spend two thirds of the time thinking what they want to hear and one third thinking about what I want to say"

— Abraham Lincoln

"Resolve to be tender with the young, compassionate with the aged, sympathetic with the striving and tolerant with the weak and wrong. Sometime in your life, you will have been all of these"

— Gautama Buddha

"There are two sides to every issue"

— Ayn Rand

"When you start to develop your powers of empathy and imagination, the whole world opens up to you"

— Susan Sarandon

"The great gift of human beings is that we have the power of empathy, we can all sense a mysterious connection to each other"

— Meryl Streep

"Empathy may be the single most important quality that must be nurtured to give peace a fighting chance"

— Arundhati Ray

"Learning to stand in somebody else's shoes, to see through their eyes, that's how peace begins. And it's up to you to make that happen. Empathy is a quality of character that can change the world"

— Barack Obama

"One friend, one person who is truly understanding, who takes the trouble to listen to us as we consider a problem, can change our whole outlook on the world"

— E. H. Mayoli

"When a good man is hurt all who would be called good must suffer with him"

— Euripides

"If there is any one secret of success, it lies in the ability to get the other person's point of view and see things from his angle as well as your own"

— Henry Ford

"Could a greater miracle take place than for us to look through each other's eye for an instant?"

— Henry David Thoreau

"Yet, taught by time, my heart has learned to glow for other's good, and melt at other's woe"

— Homer

"Have you ever been surfing? Imagine you're on your surfboard now, waiting for the big one to come. Get ready to get carried with that energy. Now, here it comes. That's empathy. No words—just being with that energy. When I connect with what's alive in another person, I have feelings similar to when I'm surfing"

— Marshall Rosenberg

"I think we all have empathy. We may not have enough courage to display it"

— Maya Angelou

"Leadership is about empathy"

— Oprah Winfrey

"Attention is the rarest and purest form of generosity"

— Simone Weil

"If speaking is silver, then listening is gold"

— Turkish proverb

"Peace cannot be kept by force; it can only be achieved by understanding"

— Albert Einstein

"If speaking is silver, then listening is gold"

— Turkish proverb

InspireMyKids.com

FAIRNESS

What does the word fairness mean to you? Being fair may entail many different things—like sharing, admitting fault, playing fair, compromising, and caring. But overall, fairness is about making sure all are treated with kindness and respect.

To help you learn more about fairness and how valuable it truly is, here are some great quotes that describe just what fairness is all about:

"He who knows only his own side of the case knows little of that"

— John Stuart Mill

"We hold these truths to be self-evident, that all men are created equal"

— US Declaration of Independence

"The best index to a person's character is how he treats people who can't do him any good—and how he treats people who can't fight back"

— Abigail Van Buren

"When you've...walked through that doorway of opportunity, you do not slam it shut behind you. You reach back, and you give other folks the same chances that helped you succeed"

— Michelle Obama

"Justice cannot be for one side alone, but must be for both"

— Eleanor Roosevelt

"Do not go around saying that the world owes you a living; it owes you nothing; it was here first"

— Mark Twain

"Fair and softly goes far"

— Miguel de Cervantes

"It is not fair to ask of someone else what you are not willing to do yourself"

— Eleanor Roosevelt

"Play fair. Don't hit people. Say you're sorry when you hurt somebody"

— Robert Fulghum

"I speak to everyone in the same way, whether he is the garbage man or the president of the university"

— Albert Einstein

"Earth provides enough to satisfy every man's need, but not every man's greed"

— Mahatma Gandhi

"Whenever I hear anyone arguing for slavery, I feel a strong impulse to see it tried on him personally"

— Abraham Lincoln

"Live so that when your children think of fairness, caring, and integrity, they think of you"

— H. Jackson Brown

"Let us not seek the Republican answer nor the Democratic answer but the right answer"

— John F. Kennedy

FRIENDSHIP

Friendship is one of life's greatest gifts. Unlike some things, such as your bedtime, your friends are your choice. Starting a new friendship can be exciting, but building a great friendship takes work! Here is what being a true friend means:

- Being helpful
- Sticking up for your friends
- Offering support
- Listening well
- Sharing
- Being honest

Here are some great quotes that get at the heart of what friendship is all about:

"The best and most beautiful things in the world cannot be seen, nor touched...but are felt in the heart"

— Helen Keller

"What is a friend? A single soul dwelling in two bodies"

— Aristotle

"Nothing but heaven itself is better than a friend who is really a friend"

— Plautus

"No road is long with good company"

— Turkish proverb

"A true friend is the greatest of all blessings"

— Francois de La Rochefoucauld

A friend is someone who knows the song in your heart and can sing it back to you when you have forgotten the words"

— Anonymous

"The best mirror is an old friend"

— George Herbert

"Truly great friends are hard to find, difficult to leave, and impossible to forget"

— G. Randolf

"It's a good thing to be rich and a good thing to be strong, but it is a better thing to be beloved of many friends"

— Oliver Wendell Holmes

"The best things in life aren't things...they're your friends"

— Anonymous

HARD WORK & DOING YOUR BEST

Sometimes doing your best work or trying your hardest at something is difficult. It may have to do with trying to do something new for the first time, like a new sport or activity at school. It may have to do with doing homework for a subject that is not your favorite or is not your best.

As Hunter S. Thompson once said, "Anything worth doing, is worth doing right." And as Albert Einstein added, "We have to do the best we can. This is our sacred human responsibility."

Developing the habits of trying your hardest and doing your best work is something that will help you succeed throughout your life. Have you have ever tried to take a shortcut and do something fast, but not well? Most of the time, the result is that you need to do it over again. And then it takes twice as long!

So, take a moment to learn from the wisdom of the quotes below. There is no doubt that following this advice will serve you well in life over and over again!

"Little by little one walks far"

— Peruvian proverb

"You should always be well and bright, for so you do your best work; and you have so much beautiful work to do. The world needs it, and you must give it!"

— Marie Corelli

"We have to do the best we can. This is our sacred human responsibility"

— Albert Einstein

"I do the very best I know, the very best I can, and I mean to keep on doing so until the end"

— Abraham Lincoln

"Do your best when no one is looking. If you do that, then you can be successful at anything you put your mind to"

— Bob Cousy

"A problem is a chance for you to do your best"

— Duke Ellington

"If you try to do your best, there is no failure"

— Mike Farrell

InspireMyKids.com

"Whatever you are, be a good one"

— Abraham Lincoln

"Doing your best means never stop trying"

— Benjamin Franklin

"Just Do It"

— Nike

"The best preparation for tomorrow is doing your best today"

— H. Jackson Brown

"Don't be afraid to give your best to what seemingly are small jobs. Every time you conquer one it makes you that much stronger. If you do little jobs well, the big ones will tend to take care of themselves"

— Dale Carnegie

"If you do things well, do them better. Be daring, be first, be different, be just"

— Anita Roddick

"Doing your best at this moment puts you in the best place for the next moment"

— Oprah Winfrey

InspireMyKids.com

"You must do the thing you think you cannot do"

— Eleanor Roosevelt

"Make the most of yourself, for that is all there is of you"

— Ralph Waldo Emerson

"Do right. Do your best. Treat others the way you want to be treated"

— Lou Holtz

"No effort that we take to attain something beautiful is ever lost"

— Helen Keller

"People pretend not to like grapes when the vines are too high for them to reach"

— Margueritte de Navarre

"So early in my life, I had learned that if you want something, you had better make some noise"

— Malcolm X

"If you're not going to go all the way, why go at all?"

— Joe Namath

InspireMyKids.com

"Do the best you can in every task, no matter how unimportant it may seem at the time"

— Sandra Day O'Connor

"Advancement only comes with habitually doing more than you are asked"

— Gary Ryan Blair

"When you reach the top, keep climbing"

— proverb

"When we do the best that we can, we never know what miracle is wrought in our life, or in the life of another"

— Helen Keller

"Do more than is required. What is the distance between someone who achieves their goals consistently and those who spend their lives and careers merely following? The extra mile"

— Gary Ryan Blair

HEROISM

When you think of the word hero, who comes to mind? A firefighter? A soldier? A comic book crime fighter? Well, these do all fit into the category of hero, but many others do as well. For instance, an animal that rescues its family from a fire is most definitely a hero! So is a volunteer who quietly feeds the homeless at a soup kitchen, or a dad who endures long hours at a hard and frustrating job in order to provide for his family.

But here's the best part about heroes—you can be a hero, too, when you stand up for what is right, do what you know you should, and be the best person you can be!

To help inspire you to bring out your inner hero, here are some great quotes that highlight just what heroism is and what a wonderful impact it can have!

"Not the glittering weapon fights the fight, but rather the hero's heart"

— Anonymous

"A hero is an ordinary individual who finds the strength to persevere and endure in spite of overwhelming obstacles"

— Christopher Reeve

"The hero is one who kindles a great light in the world, who sets up blazing torches in the dark streets of life for men to see by"

— Felix Adler

"Gold is tried by fire, brave men by adversity"

— Seneca

"True heroism is remarkably sober, very undramatic. It is not the urge to surpass all others at whatever cost, but the urge to serve others at whatever cost"

— Arthur Ashe

"Those who say that we're in a time when there are no heroes, they just don't know where to look"

— Ronald Reagan

"It doesn't take a hero to order men into battle. It takes a hero to be one of those men who goes into battle"

— Norman Schwarzkopf

InspireMyKids.com

"How would you like to meet a hero today? Go out and stand up for someone who can't stand up for themself. Go out and help someone in need. Now take a look in a mirror and you will see a hero staring back at you."

— Michael Stutman

"Any man can be a father, but it takes a special person to be a dad"

— Anonymous

"The bravest sight in the world is to see a great man struggling against adversity"

— Seneca

"Promise me you'll always remember: You're braver than you believe, and stronger than you seem, and smarter than you think"

— Christopher Robin to Winnie the Pooh

HONESTY, INTEGRITY, & MAKING GOOD CHOICES

Integrity is defined as "the quality of being honest and having strong moral principles." Integrity is about making good choices. It is doing the right things for the right reason. It is about being honest with yourself and honest with others.

Sometimes you may not be sure what the right thing to do is in a situation. When this happens, you can ask yourself a few simple questions to come up with the right answer: How will this decision affect others? Am I considering how this will make other people feel? Will I be proud to tell my parents or teacher that I did this?

Doing the right thing is an incredibly important thing. It will affect your friendships, your family, your community, and your future. Little choices that you make can have big consequences for both you and others.

Following are some inspirational quotes that help explain the importance of integrity, honesty, and doing the right thing:

"Always do right. This will gratify some people and astonish the rest"

— Mark Twain

"The time is always right to do what is right"

— Martin Luther King Jr.

"The right to do something does not mean that doing it is right"

— William Safire

"Character is doing the right thing when nobody's looking"

— J. C. Watts

"If you have integrity, nothing else matters. If you don't have integrity, nothing else matters"

— Alan Simpson

"When I do good, I feel good. When I do bad, I feel bad"

— Abraham Lincoln

"Every time I've done something that doesn't feel right, it's ended up not being right"

— Mario Cuomo

InspireMyKids.com

"To know what is right and not do it is the worst cowardice"

— Confucius

"You can easily judge the character of a man by how he treats those who can do nothing for him"

— Malcolm Forbes

"Be true to your work, your word, and your friend"

— Henry David Thoreau

"No legacy is so rich as honesty"

— William Shakespeare

"If you tell the truth you don't have to remember anything"

— Mark Twain

"Be always sure you're right, then go ahead"

— Davy Crocket

"Honesty is the best policy. If I lose mine honor, I lose myself"

— William Shakespeare

"Anyone who doesn't take truth seriously in small matters cannot be trusted in large ones either"

— Albert Einstein

"A half-truth is a whole lie"

— Yiddish proverb

"The truth is good for your soul"

— Michael Stutman

"For here we are not afraid to follow the truth wherever it may lead"

— Thomas Jefferson

"There is no right way to do a wrong thing"

— Harold S. Kushner

"Truth is the most valuable thing we have"

— Mark Twain

"Be honest with other people and, just as important, be honest with yourself"

— Michael Stutman

"Honesty is the first chapter of the book of wisdom"

— Thomas Jefferson

HUMILITY

It is good to be self-confident and to always strive to be the best you can be. Yet truly successful people also try to be great in how they treat others.

For example, you may have seen an athlete score a touchdown, drop the ball, and go down on his or her knees to give thanks for the achievement. Or another player who scores but then runs around the field, calling attention to his or her achievement. One of these people is being humble and grateful, while the other is being arrogant and boastful.

Humility is about being modest and respectful–putting others before yourself. It is not calling attention to yourself or being rude. It is about gratitude. It is about good sportsmanship.

Humility is not just for the ball field; it is something to apply to every aspect of your life. It is about being courteous, saying please and thank you all the time instead of just occasionally. It is about being able to apologize to others, even if you are just slightly in the wrong. It is also about listening and being open to learning from others. Being humble is recognizing that everyone has different strengths and paying compliments to other people.

Humility is one of the most important things you can develop as a young person. Being humble makes you a better person, a better student, and a better teammate.

Here are some great quotes on the topic of humility:

"A great man is always willing to be little"

— Ralph Waldo Emerson

"Being humble means that we are not on earth to see how important we can become, but to see how much difference we can make in the lives of others"

— Gordon B. Hinckley

"Pride is concerned with WHO is right. Humility is concerned with WHAT is right"

— Ezra Taft Benson

"True humility is not thinking less of yourself; it is thinking of yourself less"

— C. S. Lewis

"On the highest throne in the world, we still sit only on our own bottom"

— Michel de Montaigne

 InspireMyKids.com

"It is unwise to be too sure of one's own wisdom. It is healthy to be reminded that the strongest might weaken and the wisest might err"

— Mahatma Gandhi

"Every person that you meet knows something you don't; learn from them"

— H. Jackson Brown

"Without humility, there can be no humanity"

— John Buchan

"It is always the secure who are humble"

— G. K. Chesterton

"A true genius admits that he/she knows nothing"

— Albert Einstein

"Life is a long lesson in humility"

— J. M. Barrie

"You shouldn't gloat about anything you've done; you ought to keep going and find something better to do"

— David Packard

InspireMyKids.com

"None are so empty as those who are full of themselves"

— Benjamin Whichcote

"Self-praise is for losers. Be a winner. Stand for something. Always have class and be humble"

— John Madden

"Build me a son who will be strong enough to know when he is weak, and brave enough to face himself when he is afraid, one who will be proud and unbending in honest defeat, and humble and gentle in victory"

— Douglas MacArthur

LEADERSHIP

Anyone can be a leader, and the world definitely needs a lot more good leaders!

What is leadership?

It is all around you and shows up in many ways. Leadership includes the following elements:

- Doing the right thing without being asked or when no one is watching
- Helping others in need
- Guiding others on the right path
- Setting a good example for others and being a good role model
- Standing up for others even when it may be hard to do

Leadership is one of the most important skills you can learn to be the best person you can be and make the world a better place. The great thing is that you have the opportunity to practice leadership every single day in your home, at school, in sports, and everywhere in between.

Good leaders are not bossy and loud. Instead, they have the following attributes:

- Good listening
- Proactivity
- Honesty
- Generosity
- Strong communication skills
- Confidence
- Fairness
- Self-control

Here are some great quotes that help define what makes a great leader and show how leadership can make you a better person:

"A leader is one who knows the way, goes the way and shows the way"

— John C. Maxwell

"If your actions inspire others to dream more, learn more, do more and become more, you are a leader"

— John Quincy Adams

"No man will make a great leader who wants to do it all himself or get all the credit for doing it"

— Andrew Carnegie

"The leaders who work most effectively, it seems to me, never say ' I.' They don't think ' I.' They think ' we,' they think ' team'"

— Peter Drucker

"Today a reader, tomorrow a leader"

— Margaret Fuller

"Good leaders must first become good servants"

— Robert Greenleaf

"Leadership and learning are indispensable to each other"

— John F. Kennedy

"I never thought in terms of being a leader. I thought very simply in terms of helping people"

— John Hume

"Leaders aren't born; they are made. And they are made just like anything else, through hard work. And that's the price we'll have to pay to achieve that goal, or any goal"

— Vince Lombardi

"Leadership is action, not position"

— Donald H. McGannon

"A good leader inspires others with confidence in him; a great leader inspires them with confidence in themselves"

— Anonymous

"The greatest leader is not necessarily the one who does the greatest things. He is the one that gets the people to do the greatest things"

— Ronald Reagan

"Example is not the main thing in influencing others. It is the only thing"

— Albert Schweitzer

"He who cannot be a good follower cannot be a good leader"

— Aristotle

"If there is no wind, row"

— Latin proverb

LIFE

Life is good. You may have seen or even own a T-shirt or hat with that saying.

So what is it that makes life good? What makes for a good life? The answer is—a lot of things!

A good life comes from having the right attitude and taking the right actions. Here a few things that make life great:

- Having fun
- Enjoying the love of family and friends
- Doing things that you love to do
- Becoming all that you can be
- Helping others
- Enjoying each moment

Here are some inspiring and famous quotes about the gift of life and how to live a good life:

"We know what we are but know not what we may be"

— William Shakespeare

"Wheresoever you go, go with all your heart"

— Confucius

"Don't cry because it's over, smile because it happened"

— Dr. Seuss

"Yesterday is history. Tomorrow is a mystery. Today is a gift. That's why we call it 'The Present'"

— Eleanor Roosevelt

"Fall seven times, stand up eight"

— Japanese proverb

"What one can be one must be"

— Anonymous

"Life is a gift"

— Anonymous

"Not only must we be good, but we must also be good for something"

— Henry David Thoreau

"You've got to do your own growing, no matter how tall your grandfather was"

— Irish proverb

"We make a living by what we get, but we make a life by what we give"

— Winston Churchill

"Row, row, row your boat. Gently down the stream. Merrily, merrily, merrily, merrily, life is but a dream"

— Alice Munro

"I am only one, but I am one. I cannot do everything, but I can do something. And I will not let what I cannot do interfere with what I can do"

— Edward Everett Hale

"Have a heart that never hardens, and a temper that never tires and a touch that never hurts"

— Charles Dickens

"May you live all the days of your life"

— Jonathan Swift

"You have brains in your head. You have feet in your shoes. You can steer yourself any direction you choose. You're on your own. And you know what you know. And YOU are the one who'll decide where to go"

— Dr. Seuss

"The time is always right to do what is right"

— Martin Luther King Jr.

"Every action in our lives touches on some chord that will vibrate in eternity"

— Edwin Hubbel Chapin

"In any moment of decision, the best thing you can do is the right thing. The worst thing you can do is nothing"

— Theodore Roosevelt

"That best portion of a good man's life. / His little, nameless, unremembered acts / Of kindness and of love"

— William Wadsworth

"Time's fun when you're eating flies"

— Kermit the Frog

"The years teach much the days never know"

— Ralph Waldo Emerson

"Why fit in when you were born to stand out?"

— Dr. Seuss

"Do a little more than you're paid to. Give a little more than you have to. Try a little harder than you want to. Aim a little higher than you think possible, and give a lot of thanks to God for health, family, and friends"

— Art Linkletter

"To live is so startling it leaves little time for anything else"

— Emily Dickinson

"Go confidently in the direction of your dreams. Live the life you have imagined"

— Henry David Thoreau

"It's good to have an end to journey toward, but it's the journey that matters in the end"

— Ursula K. Le Guin

"We grow great by dreams"

— Woodrow Wilson

"Kid, you'll move mountains"

— Dr. Seuss

"Life itself is the most wonderful fairy tale"

— Hans Christian Andersen

"To me every hour of the day and night is an unspeakably perfect miracle"

— Walt Whitman

"Life is a succession of lessons which must be lived to be understood"

— Helen Keller

"I arise in the morning torn between a desire to improve the world and a desire to enjoy the world"

— E. B. White

"To do the useful thing, to say the courageous thing, to contemplate the beautiful thing: that is enough for one man's life"

— T. S. Eliot

"Choose a job you love, and you will never have to work a day in your life"

— Confucius

PASSION & ENTHUSIASM

What are the things in school and in life that get you most excited? Maybe you like sports, animals, music, Legos, writing, cars, or helping people. Do you have something that you are passionate about? If so, you are very lucky! If not, don't worry–you just need to pay attention to what you like and dislike and be open to trying new things. Having passion and enthusiasm is key for achieving success and meaning in school and life. As Arthur Balfour once said, "Enthusiasm moves the world."

Here are other great quotes about the importance and roles of passion and enthusiasm in life:

"Find something you're passionate about and keep tremendously interested in it"

— Julia Child

"I have no special talents. I am only passionately curious"

— Albert Einstein

"Every great dream begins with a dreamer. Always remember, you have within you the strength, the patience, and the passion to reach for the stars to change the world"

— Harriet Tubman

"Feel your emotions, Live true your passions, Keep still your mind"

— Geoffrey Gluckman

"Passion is a feeling that tells you: this is the right thing to do. Nothing can stand in my way. It doesn't matter what anyone else says. This feeling is so good that it cannot be ignored"

— Wayne Dyer

"There is no passion to be found playing small—in settling for a life that is less than the one you are capable of living"

— Nelson Mandela

"Develop a passion for learning. If you do, you will never cease to grow"

— Anthony D'Angelo

"Passion is what drives us crazy, what makes us do extraordinary things, to discover, to challenge ourselves. Passion is and should always be the heart of courage"

— Midori Komatsu

"Be brave and be patient. Have faith in yourself; trust in the significance of your life and the purpose of your passion"

— Jillian Michaels

"Passion is energy. Feel the power that comes from focusing on what excites you"

— Oprah Winfrey

"Enthusiasm is one of the most powerful engines of success. When you do a thing, do it with all your might. Put your whole soul into it. Stamp it with your own personality. Be active, be energetic and faithful, and you will accomplish your object. Nothing great was ever achieved without enthusiasm"

— Ralph Waldo Emerson

"No matter what you do with your life, be passionate"

— Jon Bon Jovi

"Rest in reason; move in passion"

— Khalil Gibran

"Don't ask yourself what the world needs; ask yourself what makes you come alive. And then go and do that. Because what the world needs is people who have come alive"

— Howard Thurman

"A person can succeed at almost anything for which they have unlimited enthusiasm"

— Charles Schwab

"'Why do we have to listen to our hearts?' the boy asked, when they had made camp that day. 'Because, wherever your heart is, that is where you'll find your treasure'"

— Paulo Cohelmo

"Doing what you love isn't a privilege; it's an obligation"

— Barbara Sher

PERSEVERANCE

Oliver Goldsmith once said that "success consists of getting up just one more time than you fall." If you think about this quote, it is really a very simple concept.

However, the reality of actually getting up each time, especially that last time, can sometimes be incredibly challenging. This is the concept of perseverance, and it is one that most successful people know well. It is the drive that keeps you focused on your goals, and it is the quality that is most often the determining factor in achieving those goals!

To help inspire you to persevere toward your goals, here are some great quotes that emphasize just how valuable perseverance is!

"Perseverance is failing 19 times and succeeding the 20th"

– Julie Andrews

"Many of life's failures are people who did not realize how close they were to success when they gave up"

– Thomas A. Edison

"Every strike brings me closer to the next home run"

— Babe Ruth

"The man who moves a mountain begins by carrying away small stones"

— Confucius

"Perseverance is a great element of success. If you only knock long enough and loud enough at the gate, you are sure to wake up somebody"

— Henry Wadsworth Longfellow

"Perseverance is the hard work you do after you get tired of doing the hard work you already did"

— Newt Gingrich

"Great works are performed not by strength but by perseverance"

— Samuel Johnson

"Perseverance, secret of all triumphs"

— Victor Hugo

"Just because you fail once doesn't mean you're gonna fail at everything"

— Marilyn Monroe

"When you get to the end of your rope, tie a knot and hang on"

– Franklin D. Roosevelt

"Be like a postage stamp, stick to something until you get there!"

– Josh Billings

"The brick walls are there for a reason. The brick walls are not there to keep us out. The brick walls are there to give us a chance to show how badly we want something. Because the brick walls are there to stop the people who don't want it badly enough. They're there to stop the other people"

– Randy Pausch

"Rivers know this: there is no hurry. We shall get there some day"

– A. A. Milne

"It always seems impossible until it's done"

– Nelson Mandela

"If you add a little to a little, and then do it again, soon that little shall be much"

– Dale Carnegie

"The price of success is hard work, dedication to the job at hand, and the determination that whether we win or lose, we have applied the best of ourselves to the task at hand"

– Vince Lombardi

"Mistakes are the doorway to discovery"

– Sam Horn

"It's not that I am so smart; it's just that I stay with problems longer"

– Albert Einstein

"Desire is the key to motivation, but it's determination and commitment to an unrelenting pursuit of your goal—a commitment to excellence—that will enable you to attain the success you seek"

– Mario Andretti

"Age wrinkles the body. Quitting wrinkles the soul"

– Douglas MacArthur

"A river cuts through a rock not because of its power, but its persistence"

– Anonymous

InspireMyKids.com

"The difference between the impossible and the possible lies in a man's determination"

– Tommy Lasorda

"Even the woodpecker owes his success to the fact that he uses his head and keeps pecking away until he finishes the job he starts"

– Coleman Cox

"Dripping water hollows out stone, not through force but through persistence"

– Ovid

"Most of the important things in the world have been accomplished by people who have kept on trying when there seemed to be no hope at all"

– Dale Carnegie

"You're never a loser until you quit trying"

– Mike Ditka

"If you've never failed, it's probably because you never tried anything very difficult"

– Clint Oster

InspireMyKids.com

"You've got to get up every morning with determination
if you're going to go to bed with satisfaction"

– George Horace Lorimer

BEING PROACTIVE

Being proactive is one of the most important ingredients to achieve success in life. People who are action focused get better jobs and better grades, have more impact in the world, and have better relationships.

When you read the quotes below from many people who helped change the world for good, you can see that taking action was part of their success.

Here are just a few of the hundreds of ways you could take positive action today:

- Help a schoolmate who is being bullied.
- Do something helpful for your parents without being asked.
- Write a nice letter to someone you admire.
- Thank a veteran.
- Do an extra-credit assignment.
- Volunteer for a good cause.

The good news is that even small actions can have a huge impact on your life and the world. So don't wait!

Now here are some great quotes about the importance of being proactive:

"A thousand words leave not the same deep impression as does a single deed"

— Henrik Ibsen

"Action is the foundational key for all success"

— Pablo Picasso

"Yesterday is gone. Tomorrow has not yet come. We have only today. Let us begin"

— Mother Teresa

"Knowing is not enough. We must apply. Willing is not enough. We must do"

— Bruce Lee

"Folks who never do any more than they get paid for, never get paid for any more than they do"

— Elbert Hubbard

"Don't wait for your ship to come in, swim out to it"

— Cathy Hopkins

"Do not wait for leaders; do it alone, person to person"

— Mother Teresa

"The fact is that in order to do anything in this world worth doing, we must not stand shivering on the bank thinking of the cold and the danger, but jump in and scramble through as well as we can"

— Sydney Smith

"People who end up with the good jobs are the proactive ones who are solutions to problems, not problems themselves, who seize the initiative to do whatever is necessary to get the job done"

— Stephen R. Covey

"It will never rain roses: when we want to have more roses, we must plant more roses"

— George Eliot

"Whatever you can do, or dream you can do, begin it. Boldness has genius, power, and magic in it. Begin it now"

— William Hutchison Murray

"An ounce of action is worth a ton of theory"

— Ralph Waldo Emerson

"The best way to not feel hopeless is to get up and do something. Don't wait for good things to happen to you. If you go out and make some good things happen, you will fill the world with hope, you will fill yourself with hope"

— Barack Obama

"The future depends on what you do today"

— Mahatma Gandhi

"You are what you do, not what you say you'll do"

— C. G. Jung

"Faith is about doing. You are how you act, not just how you believe"

— Mitch Albom

"Action may not always bring happiness, but there is no happiness without action"

— William James

"Twenty years from now, you will be more disappointed by the things that you didn't do than by the ones you did do. So throw off the bowlines. Sail away from the safe harbor. Catch the trade winds in your sails. Explore. Dream. Discover"

— H. Jackson Brown Jr.

"Follow your bliss and the universe will open doors for you where there were only walls"

— Joseph Campbell

"In any moment of decision, the best thing you can do is the right thing. The worst thing you can do is nothing"

— Theodore Roosevelt

"Don't count the days, make the days count"

— Muhammad Ali

"Do what matters, now"

— Leo Babauta

"Forever is composed of nows"

— Emily Dickinson

"Life is what you make it. Always has been, always will be"

— Eleanor Roosevelt

"How wonderful it is that nobody need wait a single moment before starting to improve the world"

— Anne Frank

"It is easy to sit up and take notice. What is difficult is getting up and taking action"

— Honore de Balzac

"Set wide the window. Let me drink the day"

— Edith Wharton

"So early in my life, I had learned that if you want something, you had better make some noise"

— Malcolm X

"The smallest act of kindness is worth more than the greatest intention"

— Khalil Gibran

"Action expresses priorities"

— Mahatma Gandhi

"If you don't make a conscious effort to visualize who you are and what you want to become in life, then you empower other people and circumstances to shape your journey by default. Your silence makes you reactive vs. proactive"

— Shannon L. Alder

"I say if it's going to be done, let's do it. Let's not put it in the hands of fate. Let's not put it in the hands of someone who doesn't know me. I know me best. Then take a breath and go ahead"

— Anita Baker

Reading is fundamental. In fact, it is one of the most important ingredients to becoming all that you can be.

Reading develops your brain, provides a window into the world around you, and helps you do better in all school subjects.

Most importantly, reading can help you become not only a better student but also a better person. You can learn from the brightest people whenever and wherever you choose.

As important as reading is, did you know that eight hundred million people around the world cannot read or write, and many families (and some schools) have no books for children to read?

There are likely many children and people in your town or city that fall into this group. Maybe someday you will be in a position to help them.

In the meantime, here are some inspiring quotes that bring to life the power of reading and reveal its ability to make you a better person:

"Once you learn to read, you will be forever free"

— Frederick Douglass

"The more that you read, the more things you will know. The more you learn, the more places you'll go"

— Dr. Seuss

"I find television very educating. Every time somebody turns on the set, I go into the other room and read a book"

— Groucho Marx

"There are many little ways to enlarge your world. Love of books is the best of all"

— Jacqueline Kennedy

"Today a reader, tomorrow a leader"

— Margaret Fuller

"There is more treasure in books than in all the pirates loot on Treasure Island"

— Walt Disney

"There are worse crimes than burning books. One of them is not reading them"

— Ray Bradbury

"Reading without reflecting is like eating without digesting"

— Edmund Burke

"The reading of all good books is like conversation with the finest people of the past centuries"

— Descartes

"Reading is to the mind what exercise is to the body"

— Richard Steele

"So please, oh PLEASE, we beg, we pray, go throw your TV set away, And in its place you can install, a lovely bookshelf on the wall"

— Roald Dahl

"Reading is a discount ticket to everywhere"

— Mary Schmich

"Books are a uniquely portable magic"

— Stephen King

"No entertainment is so cheap as reading, nor any pleasure so lasting"

— Lady Mary Wortley Montagu

"To learn to read is to light a fire"

— Victor Hugo

RESPECT

Showing respect for others is one of the most important values in the world. It means showing care for another person or thing, such as the environment.

Without respect, everything around you would be less peaceful. There would be more wars, more problems, and less happiness.

You show respect in many ways every day that you may not even realize! Respect occurs when you listen to others, play fair, use good manners, wait your turn, compliment others, pick up after yourself, and treat others well.

Being respectful is one of the key ingredients to being the best person you can be. To learn more about respect, start by checking out some of these great quotes:

"Every human being, of whatever origin, of whatever station, deserves respect. We must each respect others even as we respect ourselves"

— U. Thant

"Never judge someone by the way he looks or a book by the way it's covered; for inside those tattered pages, there's a lot to be discovered"

— Stephen Cosgrove

"Leave everything a bit better than you found it"

— Anonymous

"We are all equal in the fact that we are all different. We are all the same in the fact that we will never be the same"

— C. JoyBell C.

"It's not so much the journey that's important; as it is the way that we treat those we encounter and those around us along the way"

— Jeremy Aldana

"Tolerance only for those who agree with you is no tolerance at all"

— Ray Davis

"We must learn to live together as brothers or perish together as fools"

— Martin Luther King Jr.

"Nothing of real worth can ever be bought. Love, friendship, honour, valour, respect. All these things have to be earned"

— David Gemmell

"He who loves others is constantly loved by them. He who respects others is constantly respected by them"

— Mencius

"I speak to everyone in the same way, whether he is the garbage man or the president of the university"

— Albert Einstein

"Respect is a two-way street, if you want to get it, you've got to give it"

— R. G. Risch

"Friendship—my definition—is built on two things. Respect and trust. Both elements have to be there. And it has to be mutual. You can have respect for someone, but if you don't have trust, the friendship will crumble"

— Stieg Larsson

"Respect for ourselves guides our morals; respect for others guides our manners"

— Laurence Sterne

"One of the most sincere forms of respect is actually listening to what another has to say"

— Bryan H. McGill

"The earth does not belong to us. We belong to the earth"

— Chief Seattle

"Who am I to judge what I don't understand"

— Anonymous

"A person's a person no matter how small"

— Dr. Seuss

"Give to every other human being every right that you claim for yourself"

— Thomas Paine

"So in everything, do to others what you would have them do to you"

— The Bible: Matthew 7:12

"Without feelings of respect, what is there to distinguish men from beasts?"

— Confucius

InspireMyKids.com

"I must respect the opinions of others even if I disagree with them"

— Herbert H. Lehman

"I'm not concerned with your liking or disliking me….All I ask is that you respect me as a human being"

— Jackie Robinson

"I firmly believe that respect is a lot more important, and a lot greater, than popularity"

— Julius Erving

"To be one, to be united is a great thing. But to respect the right to be different is maybe even greater"

— Bono

"It is only when you accept how different you all are, that you will be able to see how much the same you all are. Don't expect anybody to be the same as you, then you will see that you are in many ways the same as everybody"

— C. JoyBell C.

"All the events of your past have formed a lens through which you see the world. And since no one's past is exactly like anyone else's, no two people see alike"

— Sean Covey

"A fruit salad is delicious precisely because each fruit maintains its own flavor"

— Sean Covey

"Differences were meant not to divide but to enrich"

— J. H. Oldham

"Be modest, be respectful of others, try to understand"

— Lakhdar Brahimi

"Honest differences are often a healthy sign of progress"

— Mahatma Gandhi

RESPONSIBILITY

When you think of the word responsibility, what comes to mind? Getting your school assignments done on time? Helping your family with the daily chores? Watching out for your little brother or sister? Responsibility definitely means all those things, but it means something more too.

Responsibility also entails looking inside yourself and doing all you can to be your best. And when you practice responsibility, you're on your way to making your life the very best it can be! In order to inspire you, here are some fantastic quotes about responsibility, and the tremendous impact it can have!

"The time is always right to do what is right"

— Martin Luther King Jr.

"When a man points a finger at someone else, he should remember that four of his fingers are pointing at himself"

— Louis Nizer

"If you mess up, 'fess up"

— Anonymous

"When you blame others, you give up your power to change"

— Anonymous

"Never point a finger where you never lent a hand"

— Robert Brault

"If you take responsibility for yourself, you will develop a hunger to accomplish your dreams"

— Les Brown

"Though I am not always responsible for what happens to me, I am responsible for how I handle what happens to me"

— Zig Ziglar

"Winners take responsibility. Losers blame others"

— Brit Hume

"In the final analysis, the one quality that all successful people have is the ability to take on responsibility"

— Michael Korda

"The price of greatness is responsibility"

— Winston Churchill

"Mistakes are always forgivable if one has the courage to admit them"

— Bruce Lee

"Find joy in everything you choose to do. Every job, relationship, home...it's your responsibility to love it or change it"

— Chuck Palahniuk

"Every person who has changed the world has taken responsibility for something that mattered not just to them, but to mankind"

— Michael Stutman

"There are two primacy choices in life: to accept conditions as they exist, or accept responsibility for changing them"

— Denis Waitley

"With great power comes great responsibility"

— Voltaire

"Quit making excuses. Putting it off. Complaining about it. Dreaming about it. Whining about it. Crying about it. Believing you can't. Worrying if you can. Waiting until you are older. Make a plan and just do it"

— Nike

"Even a rat can take of itself"

— Walter Conklin

"It is not only for what we do that we are held responsible, but also for what we do not do"

— Moliere

"Nothing will ever change while you point the finger of blame. Out of responsibility comes possibility"

— Lisa Villa Prosen

"Leadership is about taking responsibility, not making excuses"

— Mitt Romney

"Every right implies a responsibility, every opportunity, an obligation, every possession, a duty"

— John D. Rockefeller

"After nourishment, shelter and companionship, stories are the things we need most in the world."

–Phillip Pullman

You may not yet believe it, but writing and storytelling have the power to change your life and the lives of others. Your writing skills will impact what college you go to, what career you pursue, and how much of an impact you have on the world.

Writing and storytelling are not easy. They take effort, time, practice, and the courage to begin. They provide a way to express what you love and what excites you. They are a way to escape and create the world the way you would like it be.

The sooner you understand the power of writing and storytelling, and the power of building these skills, the better off you will be.

Check out these inspiring quotes about writing and then take action with our resources below:

"No tears in the writer, no tears in the reader. No surprise in the writer, no surprise in the reader"

— Robert Frost

"Be yourself. Above all, let who you are, what you are, what you believe, shine through every sentence you write, every piece you finish"

— John Jakes

"All that I hope to say in books, all that I ever hope to say, is that I love the world"

— E. B. White

"If there's a book that you want to read, but it hasn't been written yet, then you must write it"

— Toni Morrison

"I can shake off everything as I write; my sorrows disappear, my courage is reborn"

— Anne Frank

"You don't write because you want to say something, you write because you have something to say"

— F. Scott Fitzgerald

"So the writer who breeds more words than he needs, is making a chore for the reader who reads"

— Dr. Seuss

"I kept always two books in my pocket, one to read, one to write in"

— Robert Louis Stevenson

"My aim is to put down on paper what I see and what I feel in the best and simplest way"

— Ernest Hemingway

"The most valuable of all talents is that of never using two words when one will do"

— Thomas Jefferson

"Fill your paper with the breathings of your heart"

— William Wadsworth

"Almost all good writing begins with terrible first efforts. You need to start somewhere"

— Anne Lamott

"All I need is a sheet of paper and something to write with, and then I can turn the world upside down"

— Friedrich Nietzsche

"Easy reading is hard writing"

— Nathaniel Hawthorne

"I love writing. I love the swirl and swing of words as they tangle with human emotions"

— James A. Michener

"Write the kind of story you would like to read. People will give you all sorts of advice about writing, but if you are not writing something you like, no one else will like it either"

— Meg Cabot

"The true alchemists do not change lead into gold; they change the world into words"

— William H. Gass

"Start writing, no matter what. The water does not flow until the faucet is turned on"

— Louis L'Amour

"The scariest moment is always just before you start"

— Stephen King

"If you want to be a writer, you must do two things above all others: read a lot and write a lot"

— Stephen King

"You can make anything by writing"

— C. S. Lewis

"I write to give myself strength. I write to be the characters that I am not. I write to explore all the things I'm afraid of"

— Joss Whedon

"You can't wait for inspiration. You have to go after it with a club"

— Jack London

"The most difficult thing about writing; is writing the first line"

— Amit Kalantri

"There is nothing to writing. All you do is sit down at a typewriter and bleed"

— Ernest Hemingway

CONCLUSION

We hope you found this book to be inspiring and that many of the quotes in this book spoke to you. Perhaps one of the ideas will help you or a child in your life to take positive action toward change.

We also hope that this is the beginning, not the end, of our interaction with you. If you like what you found in this book, please consider joining InspireMyKids on our journey to help children become their best and make the world a better place.

To stay abreast of new quotes that we compile, books we publish, and real-life, inspiring stories and projects for kids, please visit our website–www.inspiremykids.com–to sign up for our e-mail list and connect with us on social media.

Also, the educator section of our website includes ideas to start incorporating inspirational quotes into your school or class and access to worksheets and common core lesson plans.

Lastly, we truly welcome your feedback:

- What book would you like to see us publish next?

- How could we make this book more valuable?

- What quote topics do you want us to explore next?

- Do you have a favorite quote you would like us to include in our next edition or book?

Please send your thoughts, feedback, and ideas to info@inspiremykids.com.

Thanks again for joining us on this journey.

Mike Stutman and the IMK Team

Co-founder and Dad

www.inspiremykids.com

mike@inspiremykids.com

Made in the USA
San Bernardino, CA
02 December 2019